ch[...]

cocktails

NH
NEW
HOLLAND

First published in 2008 by New Holland Publishers (UK) Ltd
London • Cape Town • Sydney • Auckland

Garfield House	80 McKenzie Street	Unit 1	218 Lake Road
86–88 Edgware Rd	Cape Town 8001	66 Gibbes Street	Northcote
London W2 2EA	South Africa	Chatswood	Auckland
United Kingdom		NSW 2067	New Zealand
		Australia	

ISBN 978 1 84773 231 6

Senior Editor Corinne Masciocchi
Designer Sue Rose
Photographer Ian Garlick
Production Marion Storz
Editorial Direction Rosemary Wilkinson

1 3 5 7 9 10 8 6 4 2

Reproduction by Pica Digital Pte Ltd, Singapore
Printed and bound by Tien Wah Press (Pte) Ltd, Malaysia

champagne
cocktails

david biggs

contents

introduction   **6**

the making of champagne   **12**

everybody's wine   **22**

how it's done   **27**

opening the bottle   **31**

champagne sabrage   **35**

champagne widows   **39**

champagne house visits   **42**

champagne and food   **46**

cooking with champagne   **52**

cocktails   **64**

party punches   **168**

index   **188**

introduction

Madame Lily Bollinger,
Grande Dame of Champagne.

No book on champagne would be complete without quoting the wonderful Grande Dame of Champagne, Madame Lily Bollinger, who was asked what the best time was to drink champagne. Her reply was simple:

> I drink it when I am happy, and when I am sad.
>
> Sometimes I drink it when I am alone.
>
> When I have company I consider it obligatory.
>
> I trifle with it if I am not hungry, and drink it when I am.
>
> Otherwise I never touch it – unless I am thirsty.

Champagne is indeed a drink for any time, anywhere. Like so many of life's greatest pleasures, the idea behind champagne is a simple one. The art of making great champagne, however, lies in attention to detail and refinement of natural processes.

In simplified form the basic formula for making any alcoholic beverage is this:

Sugar + yeast = alcohol + carbon dioxide

Sugar comes in many forms. It is present in starches and fruit juices, honey and cane sugar and ripe grapes. Yeasts are present almost everywhere. They are found in the air, they exist in the dark moulds that coat the damp walls of wine cellars. They are present in the waxy coating that forms the bloom on a bunch of grapes.

The first wines were probably made by nature and discovered accidentally (probably with delight) by humans. All that was required for a basic wine to be created was for the yeast on the grape skins to meet the sugar inside the grape berry. A bunch of grapes falling into a natural rock pool and being crushed by the fall would soon ferment and turn into an alcoholic liquid. It would not have taken long for an inquisitive human to taste the result and find it made him happy. Wine is indeed a product of Nature.

This basic formula covers far more than mere winemaking, however. Consider the art of the bread baker for example. The reason he uses yeast is so that the mixture will ferment and the carbon dioxide will form bubbles in the rising dough. The alcohol is evaporated in the baking process but the yeast bubbles give the bread its light, airy texture.

In the making of natural table wines the grapes are crushed to allow the yeasts on the skins to come into contact with the sugars inside the berries. (In most modern wineries the natural yeast is destroyed and replaced by specially cultivated yeast strains. This is because 'wild' yeasts can produce unpredictable results, and modern drinkers want consistency.)

Whatever yeast is used, the reaction begins and the sugars are converted to alcohol. The carbon dioxide is allowed to escape via one-way seals that permit the gas to escape without allowing air to come in. The bakers want the bubbles. The winemakers want the alcohol.

Alcohol plays a dual role in wine – it makes us happy as it is a stimulant and a magnifier of moods, and it helps to preserve the wine for a long time. If we were simply to bottle unfermented grape juice it would soon spoil and become undrinkable. The sellers of bottled grape juice invariably add chemical preservatives to prevent this happening.

Some winemakers want the bubbles as well as the alcohol. These are the men and women who make that most wonderful of all wines – champagne. In the making of sparkling wines, the bubbles form an important part of the whole. They add a joyful sparkle of tiny stars that dance playfully on the tongue. (Wine enthusiasts call this the 'mousse'. In great champagnes the mousse is very fine and lasts a long time. Inferior sparkling wines have large bubbles that soon disappear.)

No wonder this greatest of all wines has been used traditionally to celebrate great occasions. We drink it to seal a contract, to celebrate a marriage, to welcome a new baby or to toast a graduation. We drink champagne to welcome a son or daughter to adulthood. Champagne is the merriest of wines and should be used to mark all the rites of passage in our lives.

But if we believe, as Madame Lily Bollinger obviously did, that all of life is a celebration, then every occasion is a time celebrate life. And what better way to do so than by raising a glass of good sparkling wine and drinking a daily toast – 'To Life'.

the making of champagne

In his bubbly operetta, Die Fledermaus, Johann Strauss has his cast sing praises to champagne:

**His Majesty we all acclaim,
King Champagne is his name.**

Champagne is indeed the king of wines – and the wine of kings.

Legend has it that the blind monk, Dom Pérignon, was working in the cellar of the monastery of Hautvillers in France, when one of the bottles exploded, sending the cork – and some of the wine – flying out. The monk tasted the delicious sparkling wine and shouted to his companions: 'Come quickly! I think I am tasting the stars'. Thus was champagne born.

Dom Pérignon died at the monastery in 1715 and is buried there. The land was bought by the house of Moët & Chandon in 1794 and in 1921 they named their prestige champagne after the famous monk, Dom Pérignon.

Opposite: Dom Pérignon tasted the stars.

There is actually some doubt whether Dom Pérignon really did discover the way to make champagne, but why ruin a great story with mere facts? What the famous monk can certainly be credited with is the introduction of cork as a stopper for wine bottles. And without a way of sealing the pressure inside the bottles there could not be sparkling wine. (The English, of course, claim it was actually an Englishman, Christopher Merret, who discovered the method of creating sparkling wine. Dom Pérignon obviously had a better publicity team.)

The production of sparkling wine is the most labour-intensive of all winemaking activities. Before it reaches the customer, each bottle of champagne is handled at least 100 times in the cellar. No wonder some premier champagnes cost an arm and at least one leg. (There are cheaper ways of putting bubbles into wine, and these will be discussed later.)

Although most wine-producing countries make sparkling wines in the time-honoured 'méthode champenoise', only those grown in the Champagne region of north-east France may legally be called champagne. The French guard this name zealously and are quick to take legal action against anybody else claiming to make champagne. Other countries have to think of their own terms to indicate their wine was made in the old traditional way.

The Spanish, for example, use the term 'cava' for their top sparkling wines, and the South Africans call their traditionally-made bubblies 'Méthode Cap Classique', or simply MCC. The Champagne area of France lies about 160 km east of Paris and consists of five 'départements': Aisne, Aube, Haute-Mame, Mame and Seine-et-Mame. The towns of Troyes, Reims and Epernay are the commercial centres of the Champagne region.

Three main grape varieties are used in the production of champagne. These are Pinot Noir, Pinot Meunier and Chardonnay. Some other varieties are sometimes included, but in such small quantities that it is not worth mentioning them here. It sometimes comes as a surprise that two of the three champagne varieties are red grapes – Pinot Noir and Pinot Meunier – while most champagnes are made white.

Pages 16–17: Pinot Noir grapes add an earthy richness to champagne.

To achieve this, the red grapes are crushed and the free-run juice, which is white, is led off and used in the winemaking. (Red wines obtain their colour from the grape skins and if there is no skin contact the juice is white.) To make pink champagne, some of the juice of the red varieties is allowed to lie on the skins for a brief time to pick up some colour. The depth of colour can be controlled by the amount of skin contact allowed. Good champagnes are normally made crisply dry, so the grapes are usually picked at a far earlier stage than those used for still wines.

Once the base wines have been made from the various grape varieties, the cellar-master selects those he or she feels will make the best possible blend for this vintage of sparkling wines. The long process of creating champagne now begins.

Before describing the many steps in the making of champagne, let's take a closer look at the bottle in which it is sold. It is unlike any other wine bottle. First of all, it is made of unusually heavy, thick glass. This is because a high pressure develops during the fermentation process and an ordinary wine bottle would simply explode. The pressure in a champagne bottle can go as high as

8 bars (up to 90 pounds per square inch!) – some four or five times the pressure in an ordinary car tyre. Next, look at the neck of the bottle. You'll see two ridges, or flanges, cast into the glass at the mouth. One of these is to retain the wire cage, which restrains the cork, and the top one is to hold a crown cap like those used on beer bottles. The reason for this will become clear.

Once the winemaker has decided on the blend of still wines (called the 'cuvée') that will be used in the champagne, it is put into the champagne bottle and a solution of yeast and sugar is added. This is called the 'liqueur de tirage'. The bottle is now sealed with a crimped-on crown cork and laid on its side.

The yeast and added sugar now begin to ferment in the sealed bottle. In the normal run of events, yeast and sugar create alcohol and carbon dioxide gas, which is usually allowed to dissipate into the air when making still wine. But in the tightly sealed environment of the champagne bottle the gas has nowhere to go. It cannot escape, so it builds up pressure and is absorbed into the wine. When all the yeast has been converted to alcohol and carbon dioxide the spent yeast cells sink to the bottom of the bottle where they lie like a puddle of beige mud.

These spent cells are known as 'the lees'. This spent yeast is what gives good champagne its 'fresh bread' character. The wine is now allowed to rest – sometimes for several years – so the yeasty flavours are absorbed into it. The winemaker is now faced with the problem of removing these yeast cells without losing the pressure of the gas inside, or the wine itself. This begins the long process of 'remuage' or 'riddling'.

In special racks the bottles are carefully twisted and tilted slightly, day after day, so the lees work their way toward the crown cork. This can take several weeks. Eventually the yeast is gathered in a little clod or plug, resting on the cap. The bottles are now taken carefully and placed, neck-down, in a bath of freezing brine. The plug of dead yeast cells becomes a solid ice cube and at this stage the cap is popped off as neatly as possible, so the yeast flies out (actually, it's quite a messy business) in a process knows as 'dégorgement'.

The bottle now has to be topped up with a 'dosage', usually of sweetish wine, sealed with a traditional champagne cork, tied down with a wire cage and covered with a foil capsule to make it look nice. Simple? No, not very.

The addition of the dosage obviously adds a small amount of sugar to the wine, and this adds to the complexity and flavour of the final product.

Sugar limits have been laid down for the labelling of champagne and the labels give an indication of sweetness or dryness. A wine labeled 'extra brut', for instance, will contain less than 6 grams of sugar per litre. The term 'brut' indicates a sugar content of less than 15 grams per litre and 'extra dry' shows the wine will have between 12 and 20 grams of sugar per litre. 'Sec' means the sugar content is between 17 and 35 grams per litre and 'demi-sec' sugar levels are between 33 and 50 grams per litre. Any sparkling wine labelled 'doux' will have a sugar content of more than 50 g per litre.

everybody's wine

**The night they invented champagne
It's plain as it could be
They thought of you and me.**

From the classic film, Gigi

Rather sadly, champagne is often regarded only as a wine for celebrations or special occasions. We drink champagne at a wedding or a 21st birthday party. We celebrate an engagement or a graduation by drinking a glass of champagne. We drink a toast to special occasions in champagne. Champagne is used to launch ships and to spray over spectators after a Formula One motor race (such a waste!). In all of these events we miss the point that champagne is a delicious and versatile drink worthy of being opened at any time and enjoyed for itself. Indeed, when it is drunk as a toast we usually fail to give it the attention it deserves. Sensible planners use cheap and boring bubbly for toasts, because they know the flavour and delicacy of a fine champagne simply won't be appreciated as guests clink glasses and call out: 'Here's health to the happy couple!'.

In truth, champagne is one of the most versatile wines

Formula One drivers show no respect for the king of wines.
Michael Schumaker wastes the good stuff.

you can buy. Its clean, crisp character enhances the flavour of almost any food you can name. Traditionally, champagne is paired with oysters, but it is just as good with any other seafood. It is often mixed with fruit juice to make an inviting brunch cocktail, so you should not be surprised to discover it goes easily with a fruit salad at the end of a meal.

Its clean, dry character makes it the perfect accompaniment to duck, chicken, pork or veal. It goes well with oriental dishes and (naturally) with most French cuisine. Whenever you're stuck for a wine to serve with a difficult dish, consider a champagne. You'll probably have a winning combination and be hailed by your guests as an innovative host.

Champagne is also the one wine that is acceptable for drinking at breakfast time. Drink a Chardonnay or a Cabernet with your morning toast and friends will probably label you a decadent drunk. But sip a tall glass of champagne at breakfast and you'll be recognised at once as a sophisticated 'bon vivant'.

Thoughtful hosts and hostesses greet their guests with a tall flute of champagne on arrival. It sets the mood for an elegant and relaxed evening and is less formal than

the traditional dry sherry. Guests who arrive early will find it comforting to stand sipping their bubbly while waiting for late-comers to arrive. This way there's no initial awkward silence. Champagne seems to start any conversation on an easy course. By the time the last guests have arrived the early arrivals will be warm friends.

Occasionally we hear people claiming that champagne gives them a hangover, but this is hardly fair when you consider the way champagne is usually served. If it's at a wedding reception or 21st birthday bash the guests might begin the party with a whisky (or two if her Dad is paying) and then follow that with several glasses of wine before it's time for the speeches. Finally the champagne glasses are passed around and everybody drinks a toast to the happy couple. The next morning heads are thumping and you hear: 'I really shouldn't drink champagne. Every time I do I get this terrible hangover'. Of course you've forgotten the whisky and the many glasses of wine you swallowed before you raised the champagne glass to your lips. It was obviously the bubbly that hurt your head. Which is simply not true, but we do like to have something to blame for our self-inflicted misery, don't we?

how it's done

Burgundy makes you think of silly things; Bordeaux makes you talk about them, and champagne makes you do them.

Jean Anthelme Brillat-Savarin

Not all sparkling wines are made by the time-honoured méthode champenoise, although the best ones certainly are. There are easier and cheaper ways of putting bubbles into wine.

The most obvious way, of course, is simply to inject carbon dioxide into the wine under pressure just before it is sealed. This is the way old-fashioned soda siphons worked and modern Soda Stream machines do the same to make soda water. Not surprisingly it is known as the 'injection method', and is used for many of the less expensive bubblies.

The winemaker creates his base wine, deciding whether it should be dry or sweet or somewhere in between, and the bottles are filled with this wine, then given a burst of carbon dioxide and sealed. It's quick and cheap and fine for sparkling wines intended for casual parties or drinking toasts. It would also be fine for Formula One racing drivers

to squirt over everybody at the end of a race, rather than waste a bottle of the good stuff.

Sparkling wines made by the injection method can never achieve the delicate, yeasty flavours obtained by leaving champagne on the lees after the initial bottling. It will always be slightly one-dimensional, but there are plenty of occasions when this is not a problem. Incidentally, it's not advisable to try to make your own sparkling wine, using your Soda Stream machine. The resulting foamy mess is not worth the effort (take this from somebody who has tried).

Between the simple injection method and the costly méthode champenoise there's a compromise method that can achieve good results in less time and with less effort than the traditional way. This is called the 'Charmat' method, or 'cuvée close'. It is named after its inventor, Eugène Charmat of Bordeaux.

In this system the base wine is placed in a large stainless steel tank that is made particularly strong to withstand considerable pressure. The wine is then inoculated with sugar and yeast and the tank sealed tightly. Secondary fermentation takes place, but the resulting carbon dioxide cannot escape, so it is absorbed into the wine, just as is the case with bottle-fermented champagne, but on a grand scale. All that remains is to bottle and seal the wine without allowing too much of the bubble to escape.

The best Charmat-produced sparkling wines come pretty close to the real thing, even offering a little of the biscuity, yeasty character, if the wine was kept under pressure for long enough to allow it to absorb some of the lees flavours. As a brunch wine, or a wine to use in a champagne cocktail, a sparkling wine made by the Charmat process probably makes sound economic sense.

opening the bottle

One of the most horrifying sights to a true wine-lover is that of the winners of a Grand Prix race abusing magnums of good champagne. To shake a bottle of bubbly and fire off the cork like a cannon, showering the contents all over the place, is sheer sacrilege. (I am told, off the record, that the actual stuff the drivers waste is just cheap fizz put into a 'big-label' bottle for dramatic effect, but it still sets a bad example.)

A French sommelier, presenting a champagne tasting at an elegant garden party in Cape Town, started his presentation with the very French utterance: 'When it is opened correctly, a champagne bottle should merely sigh, like a satisfied woman'. He then proceeded to twist the cork gently. Suddenly there was a loud bang, the cork shot out of his hand and champagne frothed out all over the table. There was a shocked moment, during which one of the guests was heard to observe: 'Oh yes! I know her!'

Like so many things, there's a proper way to open a champagne bottle. Simply popping the cork is likely to lose some of the wine and also some of the bubbles, which make champagne so special.

The correct way is to start by carefully removing the silver foil which covers the cork and its wire cage. Usually there's a little red tag which can be pulled to tear the foil neatly. Now loosen the wire cage by twisting the little ring on the side, while keeping a thumb on the top of the cork to prevent it popping out before you're ready. Always keep the cork pointed away from you and not aimed at any of your guests.

If you are right-handed, grip the cork firmly in your left hand and the bottle in your right hand (other way round for lefties, obviously). Hold the cork firmly and twist the bottle – not the cork – gently to ease the cork out. This should give you complete control of the operation and the cork should pop out gently into your hand, with a 'sigh like a satisfied etc, etc'. Have a glass or two handy to receive the wine. Pour it and allow the initial bubbles

to settle before adding a little to top up the glass. Wine should never be filled to the brim of the glass. The right amount to pour is about three-quarters of the glass, no matter what wine you're pouring.

Until you're experienced at opening champagne, you may wish to use a small towel to grip the cork after removing the wire cage. If there is an unexpected bang, the towel will muffle it and prevent major spillage.

Incidentally, NEVER use a corkscrew on a bottle of champagne, no matter how reluctant the cork may be. The pressure in the bottle is strong enough to cause serious injury if a corkscrew were to come flying out with the cork. If the cork does seem reluctant, grip it firmly with a towel and twist it out.

It's also possible to buy a special champagne bottle opener for particularly reluctant corks. These work something like old-fashioned nut-crackers and are designed to grip the cork firmly by the top, to provide extra leverage while the bottle is twisted off. They are not essential drinks-cabinet equipment, but it's rather nice to have lots of drink-related gimmicks around if you entertain regularly, and they make useful gifts for those friends who have everything.

champagne sabrage

> **I drink champagne when I win, to celebrate... and I drink champagne when I lose, to console myself.**
>
> Napoleon Bonaparte

While the accepted way of opening a bottle of champagne is to release the cork gently and quietly, some parties are best started with a bang – and the most spectacular way of doing this is by slicing the top off a bottle of champagne using a sword or sabre. Few things could be more spectacular.

Tradition has it that the act of 'sabrage' was invented by French cavalry officers, who learned they could open a bottle of bubbly by lopping off the top with their cavalry swords – much to the astonishment and delight of their admiring womenfolk. This is machismo taken to extremes.

If fact, it's all very simple, as most magic tricks turn out to be. Before telling you how it's done, a word of warning. Practise at home, using a couple of bottles of cheap, carbonated wine. Accidents can happen and the author and publisher take no responsibility for any injury. I was

once asked to do a sabrage at a party and suggested it be done outside in the garden. The host, however, insisted the ceremony should take place at the table and a sword was duly produced. The operation went smoothly and the cork and cage flew off easily, soared across the room and lodged in the distractingly deep cleavage of one of the female guests, causing minor cuts and scratches and some tears. My offers of first aid were spurned.

To understand the mechanics of sabrage, let's take a look at some of the features of a champagne bottle. It has a deep dent – or 'punt' – in the bottom to help cope with the high pressure inside. And it has a prominent ridge round the bottle neck to grip the wire cage which secures the cork.

The pressure in the bottle can be as high as 8 bars, or eight times the pressure in a family car tyre. Glass is brittle.

The point just below the cage-retaining ridge is the weak point of the bottle. This is the key to successful sabrage. The steps described here are for right-handed people,

Opposite: Anatomy of a champagne stopper: the cage, the crown cork rim and the cage-flange, the weak point to aim for when using a sword. You may wish to remove all the foil when trying sabrage for the first time.

obviously left-handers should simply switch hands. Hold the bottle in your left hand pointing away from you, and with your thumb inside the punt to secure it (and also to keep it out of the way of the sword). Take the sword in your right hand, draw it back and slide it firmly along the top edge of the bottle toward the cork. When it strikes the ridge, the shock will cause the glass to break and the pressure in the bottle will make the cork, plus cage and foil, fly out. (You may wish to remove the foil before trying it the first time, but leave the cork and wire cage in place.)

Any tiny – and potentially harmful – slivers of glass will be expelled by the pressure. After sabrage there's a spilt second of inactivity before the wine comes frothing out. This is the moment to pour the champagne into the first glass as calmly as possible. With practice it can all be done with grace and aplomb. But don't blame us if it comes unstuck. Sometimes it does.

champagne widows

**We're off to see the widows,
The wonderful widows of Fizz.**

While wine making is generally dominated by men, it is interesting to note how many champagne brands rose to fame under the guidance of women – and specifically of widows. Could it be that the widows discovered solace for their bereavement among the twinkling bubbles in a champagne glass?

Probably the best known was Mme Barbe Nicole Clicquot Ponsardin, who was widowed at the age of 27 and left in charge of a wine cellar, about which she knew very little. Obviously she was a resourceful woman and after studying the various steps in the making of champagne she devised an ingenious method of turning the bottles daily to move the spent yeast cells gently along until they rested on the cork. Her solution was to up-end a kitchen table and drill holes in it, just large enough to accommodate the necks of the champagne bottles. Her ingenious remuage racks are in use in champagne cellars around the world today and her name lives on in the label Veuve Clicquot, the Widow Clicquot.

It is after her that the top-of-the-range La Grande Dame is named.

In 1858 the Pommery Winery was a small wine shop and hardly known anywhere but in its own village. Louise Pommery, widowed at 39, took control and set about making great changes. She was obviously a natural marketer, and one of her first moves was to build attractive new structures over the existing drab cellars. Customers want to see greatness as well as taste it. She also discovered that the British enjoyed very dry champagnes and set about developing the brut style specially for the British market. Under her canny guidance the house of Pommery grew to become one of the giants of the champagne industry.

The Laurent-Perrier house owes its greatness to not one, but two widows. In the late 1800s the widowed Mathilde Emile Laurent-Perrier took over the running of the champagne business and was hugely successful until her death, after which the fortunes of the brand began to falter. The cellar was bought by another widow, Marie-Louise de Nonancourt, who raised it back to its former glory.

When businesses – and luxury businesses in particular – were hard hit by the Depression in the early 1930s,

Madame Camille Olry-Roederer found herself at the helm of the family business which consisted not only of a champagne cellar, but a thoroughbred horse stud as well. Under her guidance the business prospered and her top-of-the range Cristal champagne is the favourite of celebrities the world over, including the British Royal family.

But the most quoted of all the champagne widows is undoubtedly Madame Lily Bollinger, whose famous 'I drink it when I am happy…' quotation is probably the motto of every champagne maker in France. She took over the winery in 1941 and soon doubled the production of the cellar. Under her guidance Bollinger became one of the most recognised champagne labels in the world.

champagne
house visits

Chateau Bollinger is almost a sacred shrine to visiting champagne lovers.

The word champagne can refer both to the area of France in which the famous drink is produced, as well as to the wine itself. Many countries produce sparkling wines using a similar method, but only those from the Champagne region may legally be called champagne. The region is situated about 150 km east of Paris and the unique character of real champagne comes partly from the chalky soil in the Champagne region, as well as the ideal climate for growing the champagne grape varieties.

Most of France's famous champagne houses offer cellar tours at reasonable prices, and these usually end with a tasting of the cellar's products. Some are quite spectacular, being set deep underground in the ancient Roman chalk mines, known as 'crayères'. Some of the chalk walls of these caves have been carved into elaborate relief sculptures.

During the tour you will probably be shown all the stages in the long process of creating champagne – from the large stainless steel tanks in which the still wine is stored prior to blending, the racks of millions of bottles of champagne being riddled each day and the caves of stored champagne undergoing its long maturation.

You will probably also be given a demonstration of 'dégorgement', where the frozen plug of spent yeast is removed from the bottles. In each case the process is similar, so you'll probably want to do only one or two cellars during a visit to the Champagne region.

Some champagne houses require visitors to make a prior appointment to be taken on a tour, and this may be the best way to visit, rather than finding yourself being swept along with the members of a large coach tour. Most of the great champagne houses have their own websites, so it should be easy to arrange your visits online.

A list of the region's top champagne brands would include the following:

Moët & Chandon   **Pommery and Greno**
Bollinger   **Louis Roederer**
Veuve Cliquot   **Pol Roger**
GH Mumm   **Mercier**
Piper-Heidsiek   **Krug**
Taittinger   **Henriot**
Perrier-Jouet   **Billecart-Salmon**
Laurent-Perrier

Of course there are many more, some offering incredibly good champagne at prices far more affordable than those of the great labels. Any visit to the Champagne region should turn into a voyage of wine discovery.

One of the most popular cellar tours for visitors is that offered by Mercier. The visitors' centre was built around what is claimed to be the world's largest barrel. It was built in 1889. Here the visitors are given a short video production before being taken by lift 30 metres down into the cellars. From here there's a laser-guided train tour along the 18 kilometres of chalk galleries. The tour ends with a champagne tasting in the souvenir shop.

Another spectacular tour is offered by Pommery, in Reims. Here visitors descend the 101 steps into 18 kilometres of cellar galleries, created from what were once ancient Roman chalk pits. They are said to contain more than 20 million bottles.

Whichever champagne house you choose to visit, you can be assured of an interesting insight into the making of the king of wines, and also a tasting and the chance to buy a bottle or two to take home.

champagne and food

Before I was born my mother was in great agony of spirit and in a tragic situation. She could take no food except iced oysters and champagne. If people ask when I began to dance, I reply, 'In my mother's womb, probably as a result of the oysters and champagne – the food of Aphrodite'.

Isadora Duncan, the famous dancer

Some people would claim that champagne should be enjoyed on its own. Champagne is perfection and needs no help from food, they say. Others say champagne is the most versatile wine there is and it goes well with almost any food. Oysters are a natural partner for this king of wines, but there are other sublime combinations. Let's explore some possibilities.

First of all, let's remember that champagnes come in several styles, from demi-sec to extra brut. Some champagnes will obviously pair better with certain foods than others. It should also be remembered that general terms like poultry, seafood and red meat cover a multitude of flavours.

Opposite: Romantic dancer Isadora Duncan claimed she learned to love champagne in her mother's womb.

With modern high-production farming methods, foods simply do not taste as full-flavoured as they once did. To cover up for this diminished flavour, cooks usually add a sauce to the dish and each dish gets its character from the sauce in which it was cooked, so a chicken breast poached in lemon juice is completely different from one baked in a creamy mushroom sauce, although both are undoubtedly poultry. The real test is to decide whether the dish is heavy or light in flavour, and match it with an equivalent 'weight' of wine.

Vintage champagnes are made from the finest grapes harvested in a single vintage year. They are aged for a long time on the lees, with the result they are richer and more complex than non-vintage champagnes. These full-flavoured wines can be paired with rich foods like pâtés, smoked salmon, caviar and crispy roast duck. It is one of the few wines that goes well with creamy sauces.

Brut non-vintage champagne is dry and crisp in character and can handle a wide range of foods, from breakfast to dinner. Try one with scrambled eggs at a brunch, for example, or with grilled mushrooms, hard cheeses like parmesan, pasta, thin-crust pizza or almost any seafood or chicken dish.

Extra brut champagne is bone dry and has not been given any sweet dosage before bottling. It goes well with risotto and sometimes with crispy roast duck. Its clean, crisp flavour makes it the perfect foil to oysters or caviar. It can also be served as a palate-cleanser between main courses at a formal dinner.

Blanc de Blancs are made from Chardonnay without the addition of the traditional Pinot Noir. They are not as complex as some other styles, but their clean, crisp character goes well as an aperitif before a meal. They're also perfect for lighter foods, like salads, uncomplicated seafood and chicken dishes.

Demi-sec champagnes are the sweetest of the champagnes and are sometimes served at the end of a meal with chocolate, soft cheese, not-too-sweet dessert or coffee, instead of the more traditional port.

Blancs de Noirs champagne is made from only the red grape varieties, Pinot Noir and Pinot Meunier. It usually has a deep golden colour and full flavour and goes best with full-flavoured foods like cheeses, pasta and red meat dishes. It will probably make a good partner for venison.

Rosé champagne is made from the red grape varieties and has been given just enough skin contact to turn it a delicate and romantic shade of pink. These are perfect lunch-time wines and go well with summer foods like shaved smoked ham, green salads, cold chicken or Greek salad. Rosé champagne can be served as a good accompaniment to pheasant and guinea fowl. Pink champagne also has romantic connotations and is said to be a good aphrodisiac if used thoughtfully. An evening with candlelight and pink champagne is almost sure to end lovingly. Sales of pink champagne usually soar in February, when lovers celebrate St Valentine's Day.

cooking with champagne

Wine has always been regarded as an essential ingredient of good cooking. This seldom extends to champagne, because cooking destroys the bubbles, and that rather removes the whole point of champagne, doesn't it? There are, however, some recipes in which the subtle, yeasty flavour of champagne forms an important part, even without the bubbles. There are also occasions when, after a party, the host finds a left-over glass or two of champagne at the bottom of the bottle. It seems a pity to throw it away, so it may as well be used for cooking. Here are a few recipes to try.

champagne, peach and melon soup

Here's a deliciously refreshing dish to start a light summer lunch on the terrace. It's also a chance to use any of those old-fashioned saucer-shaped champagne glass you may have tucked away. Although it does not involve any actual cooking, it certainly provides a tasty treat.

Ripe, sweet melon

2 large ripe peaches per serving

Bottle of champagne

Sprigs of mint, to garnish

Remove the melon skin and seeds and cut the flesh into cubes. Peel the peaches and remove the stones. Place all the fruit in a blender and blend to a smooth purée. Store this in the fridge until just before serving.

When needed, pour the purée into the glasses, filling them to about the halfway mark. Top up with freshly opened champagne, stir very lightly and garnish with sprigs of mint.

champagne oysters

Champagne and oysters are natural companions and often served together, usually with the oysters raw in the shell. In this recipe the relevant flavours are brought closer together. It takes about half an hour to prepare and 10 minutes to cook.

115 g/4 oz (½ cup) unsalted butter

2 shallots, finely chopped

½ bottle of pink champagne

Salt and black pepper, to taste

2 tsp fresh chopped tarragon

Dozen oysters, opened

Tarragon leaves, to garnish

Place half the butter in a pan and once it is hot, fry the shallots in it for about a minute. Now add the champagne, seasoning and tarragon and bring to the boil, stirring occasionally. Simmer under the liquid is reduced to about half its volume.

Add the oysters to the mixture and cook for two minutes, then remove each oyster and place it back in a shell.

Now increase the heat, add the remaining butter and blend it thoroughly with a whisk. Pour the sauce over the oysters, garnish with the tarragon leaves and serve immediately.

champagne chicken breasts

You'll need about 230 ml/8 fl oz (1 cup) of champagne for this recipe, and it doesn't matter if it's gone flat. It's the flavour, not the bubbles, that makes the difference here.

2 de-boned skinless chicken breasts

4 Tbsp butter

50 g/2 oz / ½ cup finely chopped fennel

40 g/½ oz (½ cup) finely chopped mushrooms

115 ml/4 fl oz (½ cup) chicken stock

Flour, for dusting

230 ml/8 fl oz (1 cup) champagne

230 ml/8 fl oz (1 cup) fresh cream

Salt and black pepper, to taste

Cut the chicken breasts in half, to make four pieces, and flatten with a meat mallet or rolling pin until they are about 1 cm (⅜ in) thick.

Take half the butter, place it in a large frying pan and sauté the fennel and mushrooms for about a minute. Add the chicken stock and simmer for a few more minutes.

Move the vegetables and sauce to one side of the pan, dust the chicken pieces lightly with flour and place them in the pan with the remaining butter. Cook for about a minute each side, move the vegetables back to surround the chicken, then pour the champagne over. Allow it to come to the boil, then add the fresh cream, stir and season if necessary, and serve immediately.

champagne ham glaze

It's hardly likely that you'd be happy to open a fresh bottle of good champagne simply to make a glaze for your Christmas ham. It is, however, quite possible that you have some champagne left over from a pre-Christmas party. It will probably be too flat to drink now, but that doesn't matter if you're going to use it for cooking. Let's presume you have about three-quarters of a bottle of flat champagne to use.

1 ham joint

¾ bottle of champagne

400 g/14 oz (2 cups) brown sugar

1 Tbsp honey

1 tsp ground ginger

1 tsp dry mustard powder

Pineapple slices, to garnish

Place the ham on a rack in a baking pan and score it with a sharp knife.

Now combine the champagne, brown sugar, honey, ginger and mustard powder in a saucepan and bring to the boil, stirring constantly. When it has formed a sticky syrup, pour it over the ham and set it in the oven to bake as usual.

Open the oven occasionally and baste the ham with the syrup until done. You may like to garnish the dish with slices of pineapple before serving.

pomegranate sorbet with bubbles

In this pudding recipe the champagne bubbles form part of the charm. It all adds up to a delicious palate cleanser at the end of a good meal. You will need an ice-cream maker for this dish.

200 g/7 oz (1 cup) sugar

230 ml/8 fl oz (1 cup) water

485 ml/17 fl oz (2 cups) red pomegranate juice, preferably freshly squeezed and strained

2 tsp fresh lemon juice

Bottle of chilled demi-sec champagne

Seeds of 1 pomegranate, to garnish

In a saucepan over a medium heat, combine the sugar with the water and simmer until reduced to about 170 ml / 6 fl oz (¾ cup) syrup. Allow to cool to room temperature and stir in the pomegranate juice and lemon juice.

Place the mixture in the ice-cream machine and follow the maker's instructions to make sorbet.

When it is done, transfer it to the freezer until needed. It should last for up to three days. To serve the dessert, place a scoop of the sorbet in a small pudding bowl, pour some champagne around it and garnish with a sprinkling of pomegranate seeds.

cocktails

SHED ICE
HALF A
GE GLASS
ASCO
HRE
NTO
OF SALT
WITH

37.5% v

> **Champagne and orange juice is a great drink. The orange improves the champagne and the champagne definitely improves the orange.**
>
> Philip, Duke of Edinburgh

Champagne has been used for many years to add sparkle to a cocktail. Some traditional drinkers say this is close to sacrilege. Anything added to a champagne can only diminish its royal flavour, they claim.

In the modern world, however, the status of royalty is not as sacred as it once was, so there's less indignation about mixing champagne than there may once have been. A good compromise would be to use a sparkling wine of lesser breeding – a bubbly made by the Charmat method, for example. A German Sekt, an Italian Prosecco or a Californian sparkling wine would be ideal.

Only the most pretentious of wine connoisseurs would suggest they can still taste the finer nuances of a good champagne once it has been mixed with fruit juice and other flavourings. In these recipes we shall use the term champagne throughout. If it offends you, please substitute sparkling wine. The result will be almost as delicious.

One thing that all champagne-based cocktails recipes have in common is that they are not shaken or stirred like most other mixed drinks. One of the reasons for adding champagne is to get the sparkle, and shaking or stirring it will soon release all the bubbles, leaving you with a flat drink. Pour it carefully and slowly and you'll get it all.

Exact measurements are not given here, as they will vary from one drinker to another, according to taste. The term 'bar measure' means about 30 ml, or 1 fl oz – or 1 egg-cup full. Let's not be pedantic.

One good feature of champagne-based drinks is that they usually require a minimum of bar equipment. The drinks are not shaken or stirred, so there's no cocktail shaker required. Champagne drinks are not often served with ice, so you do not even need an ice bucket.

Warm cocktails of any sort are an abomination, however, so all the ingredients should be used as cold as possible. Keeping the various bottles in the fridge overnight should do the trick. It's also a good idea to chill the glasses to be used. This is best done by leaving them in the fridge or freezer for a few hours before they are needed.

buck's fizz

Probably the best known of all champagne-based drinks, Buck's Fizz is traditionally served at breakfasts, brunches and gentlemanly sporting events. Many of the other champagne cocktails are simply variations of this basic recipe of orange juice and champagne, with additions.

Champagne

Orange juice (preferably freshly-squeezed)

Ice cubes

Place a few ice cubes in a tall glass and cover with fresh orange juice, filling the glass to about one-fifth. Carefully pour chilled champagne over it to fill the glass, and serve.

kir royal

Like so many famous foods and drinks, this one has its origins among the peasants. In the 19th century, farm workers in Burgundy, France, led a hard life. Part of the reward for their labours came in the form of a regular hand-out of wine. Of course, the farmer was not likely to waste his good stuff on unappreciative peasants, so the daily dole was usually of a very poor quality. The labourers, however, improved the situation by adding the blackcurrant-flavoured cassis syrup to their wine to make it less rough. They named this concoction kir, after the mayor of Dijon, Canon Felix Kir, highly admired as a war hero. Later the drink became fashionable among the rich folk, and connoisseurs improved it by using champagne instead of rough wine. They also used crème de cassis liqueur, instead of the cassis syrup. This elevated it to royal status and the drink became known as Kir Royal.

1 bar measure (about 30 ml/1 fl oz) crème de cassis

Champagne

Simply pour the crème de cassis into a tall champagne flute and top up carefully with chilled champagne.

black velvet

It is not generally known that this popular drink had its origin in a time of deep mourning. Queen Victoria plunged the whole of England into official mourning after the death of her beloved Prince Albert. The barman in Brooks' Club in London certainly entered into the spirit of sorrow and in 1861 he allegedly decided that even the champagne he served should go into mourning. He started serving his Black Velvet drinks, which consisted of equal quantities of champagne and Guinness stout. The original Black Velvets were served in beer tankards, but as the drink gained genteel acceptance, it became acceptable to serve it in a champagne flute.

½ glass Guinness

Champagne

Half fill a glass with Guinness and then carefully trickle the chilled champagne onto it to disturb the bubbles as little as possible.

brunch bubbly

There are many versions of tall cocktails containing champagne and fruit juice. This one was developed to suit the warm summer mornings on the Cape Peninsula in South Africa. It can be modified to accommodate whatever fruit is in season at the time. Mid-morning brunch has become a popular weekend social occasion for friends in the Cape, as it is often uncomfortably hot by lunch-time and nobody wants to wait until evening before enjoying a convivial drink. The Brunch Bubbly can be partly prepared the evening before the gathering.

Bowl of fresh, ripe strawberries

Bottle of brandy

Slice a number of large, juicy ripe strawberries into halves, place them in a small bowl and cover with brandy. Leave in the fridge overnight.

Peach juice (fresh if possible)

Bottle of chilled champagne

Shortly before the guests arrive, place half a brandied strawberry in each champagne flute, together with enough of the brandy to cover it. Now pour in peach juice until the glass is about one-third full.

When the guests arrive, pop a bottle of chilled champagne and top up each glass to provide a refreshing start to the day.

champagne martini

It had to happen, of course. Every cocktail recipe book contains at least one martini recipe. There are literally hundreds of different versions of the martini, and whole books have been written on the subject. In this case champagne is used instead of the original vermouth. A red berry takes the place of the traditional olive.

1 bar measure (about 30 ml/1 fl oz) vodka

Champagne

Mulberries or raspberries

Pour the vodka into a champagne flute, top up with champagne and drop in one or two berries as garnish. This martini should definitely be stirred and not shaken, but do it very gently to preserve the bubbles.

tangerine treat

Simple is often best and this simple blend of champagne and fruity juice is, as the name suggests, a real treat. Tangerine is a member of the citrus family, so this is really just a variation of the classical Buck's Fizz.

½ glass tangerine juice

Dry champagne

Half fill a champagne flute with tangerine juice and top it up gently with chilled champagne.

caribbean champagne

Any drink that claims to be Caribbean will have the flavours of tropical fruit in it. This is no exception.

1 tsp crème de banane liqueur

1 tsp white rum

Dash of orange bitters

Dry champagne

Place the banana cream, rum and bitters in a champagne flute and carefully top with champagne, then stir very gently.

ruby royale

Chambord is a black raspberry liqueur made in France. In this recipe it is used to add a touch of power to raspberry purée, with vodka adding the final kick.

About 1 cup fresh raspberries

1 bar measure (about 30 ml/1 fl oz) Chambord

1 bar measure (about 30 ml/1 fl oz) vodka

Champagne

Keep one raspberry as a garnish and whizz the remaining raspberries in a blender to make a smooth purée. Place the Chambord and vodka in a tall (highball) glass and half fill with raspberry purée. Stir well and gently top with chilled champagne. Garnish with the remaining berry.

champagne julep

Traditionally, a julep is a long drink containing sugar, spirit and mint, and served in a tall, frosted glass. It became popular in America's Southern States when plantation owners used it to combat the heat of the summer. Champagne, of course, turns the julep into a royal treat.

2 sprigs of fresh mint

Sugar cube

1 Tbsp brandy

Ice cubes

Champagne

Slices of fresh fruit, to garnish

Place the mint and sugar cube in a tall glass and soak in brandy. Now add three ice cubes and slowly fill the glass with champagne. Stir gently and decorate with a few slices of fresh fruit.

champagne normande

Calvados is the spirit distilled in Normandy from apples. It adds a fine fiery note to the clean flavour of champagne. The bitters and sugar add flavour without upsetting the balance of the drink.

Sugar cube

1 Tbsp calvados

Dash of Angostura bitters

Chilled champagne

Slice of orange, to garnish

Place the sugar cube in a champagne flute, add the calvados and bitters, and stir until the sugar has dissolved. Top up the glass gently with chilled champagne and add the slice of orange to garnish.

alfonso

Closely related to the Classic Champagne Cocktail (see page 90) is the Alfonso, which is said to have been named after King Alfonso XIII of Spain, who was deposed and spent his exile in France in the early 20th century. This was reputed to be one of his favourite drinks. Dubonnet is one of France's most widely advertised drinks, so its inclusion should not come as a surprise. Dubonnet is an astringent wine-based drink made from Carignan, Grenache and Malvoise Muscat grapes flavoured with quinine and bitter bark. The resulting cocktail is drier than the Classic and has a very clean finish. It makes a perfect aperitif.

Sugar cube

Few dashes of Angostura bitters

1 bar measure (about 30 ml/1 fl oz) Dubonnet

Champagne

Twist of lemon

Place the sugar cube in a champagne flute and add a few dashes of Angostura bitters. Pour in the Dubonnet and top up with the champagne, gently poured to retain the bubbles. Squeeze the twist of lemon over the drink, and serve ungarnished.

classic champagne cocktail

The Brunch Bubbly described on page 74 is closely related to the Classic Champagne Cocktail in that it recognises the comfortable relationship between sparkling wine and brandy – both being children of the grape. As in all good cocktails the secret lies in finding the perfect balance between sweet and sour flavours.

Sugar cube

Several dashes of Angostura bitters

1 bar measure (about 30 ml/1 fl oz) Cognac or good brandy

Champagne

Maraschino cherry, to garnish (optional)

Place the sugar cube in a tall champagne flute and splash a few dashes of Angostura bitters on to it. Add the Cognac and top up carefully with chilled champagne. The drink is sometimes garnished with a maraschino cherry on a cocktail stick.

bellini

This classic champagne cocktail was created in Harry's Bar in Venice. It is best made using very ripe peaches, but when these are not available it is acceptable to use ready-made peach juice instead.

Equal quantities of peach juice and champagne

Peal and quarter the peaches, and remove the stones. Place the peach quarters in a blender to create a smooth peach juice. This can be done in advance and the juice kept in the fridge for a day or two before being needed.

When ready to serve, half-fill a champagne flute with the peach juice and carefully top up with well chilled champagne. If you'd prefer the two to blend before serving, stir carefully, trying not to dissipate too many of the precious bubbles.

london special

The British have a taste for slightly bitter drinks. A dash of bitters is used to create the popular 'pink gin' and in every London pub you'll hear the standard order: 'a pint of bitter, please'. So it's hardly a surprise to find that Londoners added an element of bitterness to their champagne to make it their own.

Sugar cube

2 dashes of Angostura bitters

Twist of orange

Chilled brut champagne

Place the sugar cube in a chilled champagne glass and splash two dashes of bitters onto it. Drop the twist of orange into the glass and top it up gently with chilled champagne.

nelson's blood

With a name like this, Nelson's Blood is an appropriate cocktail to serve at a nautical occasion – possibly the prize-giving at the end of a sailing regatta, or simply as a sundowner on the deck of a yacht, rocking gently at anchor.

Tawny Port

Champagne

To make it, pour about one-fifth of a champagne flute of Tawny Port and top up the glass with chilled champagne, running it carefully down the side of the glass to preserve the bubbles.

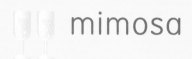 # mimosa

This popular brunch drink is a spiced-up version of the classic Buck's Fizz (see page 68), with the addition of a splash (or more, depending on taste) of triple sec (a very sweet white curaçao).

Orange juice

Champagne

Triple sec

Pour about one-fifth of a champagne flute of orange juice, fill almost to the top with chilled champagne and then trickle the triple sec over to it. Serve un-stirred.

death in the afternoon

This drink, named after Ernest Hemingway's novel, was originally made with absinthe, the liquor which is banned in some countries, but traditionally enjoyed by the French Impressionist painters. While absinthe is making a comeback internationally, it will probably be easier to substitute another anise-flavoured drink, such as Pernod.

Absinthe or Pernod

Champagne

Simply pour about one-fifth of a chilled champagne flute of absinthe and top up gently with chilled champagne, taking care not to lose too many of the bubbles.

chambord royale spritzer

Chambord (full name Chambord Liqueur Royale de France) is a delicious black raspberry liqueur made in France. This spritzer is usually made as a low-alcohol long summer drink, but of course many variations are possible. By cutting down on the club soda and increasing the champagne it can become quite a powerful drink. Here is the original version.

Ice cubes (optional)

Chambord Royale

Champagne

Club soda

Place three or four ice cubes in a tall glass and pour in enough Chambord to cover them. Fill the glass to halfway with champagne and top up with club soda.

americana

Few drinks capture the American spirit more accurately than bourbon whiskey, so it's not surprising to find that serious American drinkers use their favourite liquor to add extra oomph to their champagne.

1 Tbsp bourbon

Dash of orange bitters

½ tsp caster sugar

Dry champagne

Slice of ripe peach soaked overnight in brandy, to garnish

Stir the bourbon, orange bitters and caster sugar together in a mixing glass (a wine glass will do well here) and once the sugar has dissolved, pour it into a tall champagne flute. Top up carefully with chilled champagne, trying not to let it froth too much, and garnish with the slice of brandy-soaked peach.

imperial fizz

Closely related to the Americana (see page 104), the Imperial Fizz uses lemon juice instead of the orange bitters and is even simpler to make. The result, however, is quite different.

Crushed ice

½ tsp caster sugar

Sherry-glass of bourbon

Half as much fresh lemon juice

Brut champagne or dry sparkling wine

Place a cup of crushed ice in a cocktail shaker and add the caster sugar, bourbon and lemon juice. Shake well and strain into a champagne flute. Top up with chilled champagne and serve.

 eve

In spite of its name, this was probably *not* the first drink to be created. It does have a pretty pink blush to it, which could have reminded its inventor of all things gentle and feminine.

Splash of Pernod

Sherry-glass of Cognac

2 tsp caster sugar

2 tsp curaçao

Ice cubes

Chilled pink champagne

Pour the Pernod into a wine glass and swirl it around to coat the sides of the glass. Add the Cognac to the glass. In a small bowl or separate glass combine the sugar and curaçao and stir to dissolve the sugar, then add to the wine glass and stir well. Add two ice cubes and top up with chilled pink champagne.

king's peg

A 'peg', in drinking terms, is a measure of liquor. In early days in Britain the drinking vessels were marked on the inside with small studs (or 'pegs') to indicate the various quantities. Drinkers would order 'a peg of rum', or 'two pegs, please'. Any drink that contained champagne was likely to be regarded as being fit for a king, so it was natural to call this one the King's Peg.

Ice cubes

Sherry-glass of Cognac

Chilled brut champagne

Place two or three ice cubes in a large wine glass and add the Cognac. Gently top up with champagne, trying not to lose too many bubbles.

tintoretto

The connection between the classical painter, Tintoretto, and a pear-based drink is not clear, but both certainly provide pleasure in their own spheres. Maybe the name, in this case, is unimportant.

1 dessertspoon of puréed pear

Chilled champagne

Splash of pear brandy

Place the pear purée in a champagne flute and top up with champagne. Carefully dribble a few dashes of pear brandy on the top and serve.

amaretto ritz

Amaretto is a liqueur made from almonds and is a useful flavour to add to cocktails. In this recipe, a touch of blue adds mystery while the lemon juice balances the sweetness of the amaretto.

Splash of amaretto

1 tsp blue curaçao

Dash of lemon juice

Dry champagne

Twist of lemon peel, to garnish

Splash the amaretto, curaçao and lemon juice into a tall champagne flute and carefully fill it with chilled champagne. You may like to decorate it with a twist of lemon peel.

prince of wales

Down the years there have been many Princes of Wales — some of impeccable character and others with a very dubious reputation for riotous living. We don't know which one made this drink, but the recipe looks as though the inventor took a fairly standard cocktail and simply added a good measure of champagne to turn it into a longer drink. Come to think of it, what's wrong with that?

Ice cubes

About 1 egg-cup of Madeira wine

Equal quantity of brandy or Cognac

3–4 drops curaçao

2 dashes of Angostura bitters

Champagne

Slice of orange, to garnish

Place four or five ice cubes in a cocktail shaker and add the Madeira, brandy, curaçao and bitters. Shake well and strain into a champagne flute, top up with chilled champagne and garnish with a thin slice of orange.

pimm's royale

Many fine summer drinks are made simply by adding a splash of flavouring to a glass of champagne. Pimm's No 1 is a gin-based spirit flavoured with fruit-based liqueurs and often served garnished with a whole range of fresh fruits. Turn it into a Pimm's Royale to make a deliciously dry summertime drink.

Champagne

Splash of Pimm's No 1

Spear of cucumber, to garnish

Pour three-quarters of a flute of champagne, add a generous splash of Pimm's and garnish with a long spear of fresh cucumber.

the ghost

Here's another simple champagne-based drink that consists mainly of champagne, with just a splash of flavouring. In this case the sweetness of the melon liqueur is perfectly balanced by the dryness of the champagne.

Glass of brut or extra brut champagne

Splash (about 1 Tbsp) of Midori melon-flavoured liqueur

To make it, simply fill a chilled champagne flute almost to the top and add a splash of Midori. What could be simpler?

champear

In this easy-to-make champagne drink the flavour is floated gently on top, trying not to allow the two ingredients to mix. This gives you the aroma of the pears before you discover the freshness of the champagne.

Glass of brut champagne

1 bar measure (about 30 ml/1 fl oz) pear brandy

Pour the champagne into a chilled flute and allow the foam to settle before gently floating the pear brandy on the top. The first mouthful gives you a smack of fiery liquor and aromatic pear flavour and this is followed by the cooling champagne.

poinsettia

This is a very attractive looking drink that tastes as good as it looks. The complex berry and orange flavours are perfectly offset by the dryness of the champagne.

1 bar measure (about 30 ml/1 fl oz) cranberry juice

Half that quantity of triple sec

Glass of dry champagne

Twist of lime

Pour a splash of triple sec and two splashes of cranberry juice into a chilled champagne flute and top up carefully with champagne, pouring a little at a time to prevent excessive frothing. Squeeze the twist of lime over the drink and drop it in as garnish.

d'artagnan

D'Artagnan is probably best known as one of the Three Musketeers, but the original D'Artagnan is the patron saint of the Armagnac region of France. To honour the saint it might be polite to use Armagnac brandy in this drink, but any fine brandy will do.

1 tsp Armagnac brandy

1 tsp Grand Marnier

1 tsp sugar syrup

4 tsp fresh orange juice

Dry champagne

Peel of 1 orange, to garnish

You may wish to make enough of this delicious drink to serve four or five guests, so pour the brandy, Grand Marnier, sugar syrup and orange juice in the correct proportions into a jug and chill overnight in the refrigerator.

When required, pour the required amount into a chilled champagne flute and top up carefully with champagne. Cut the orange peel into thin strips and use as garnish.

french 75

This classic champagne cocktail is found in almost every book of drinks recipes and was probably named after a famous field gun. It can be made to any calibre to suit your palate. There are two versions – one based on gin and the other on brandy. Both are well worth trying.

FOR THE GIN VERSION

Cracked ice

About 1 sherry-glass of dry gin

Juice of ½ lemon

1 tsp caster sugar

Champagne

Twist of lemon peel, to garnish

Fill a tall glass with cracked ice and add the gin, lemon juice and caster sugar. Stir to dissolve the sugar and top up with champagne. Garnish with the twist of lemon peel.

For the brandy version, simply substitute brandy for the gin in the above recipe.

royal screw

The naming of mixed drinks is often an interesting business. The old Screwdriver is a classic example. For obvious reasons construction workers on New York's skyscrapers were strictly forbidden to take alcohol on site with them. This didn't stop the die-hards, who used to take a bottle of orange juice laced with vodka to work. 'What's that in your lunch pail?' the boss would ask. 'Oh just a screwdriver' came the answer. Substitute champagne and Cognac for the vodka and you have a right royal screw.

Sherry-glass of Cognac

Sherry-glass of orange juice (freshly squeezed if possible)

Dry champagne

Pour the Cognac and orange juice into a chilled wine glass, stir and add the chilled champagne to fill the glass.

champagne flip

Flips are creamy cocktails that include egg yolk to add a creamy smoothness. They are sometimes administered as medicines and are reputed to fend off all manner of ailments. Of course, they have the benefit of being tasty as well. You don't have to wait for a touch of flu to enjoy this one.

Ice cubes

1 Tbsp brandy

1 tsp Cointreau

2 tsp fresh cream

1 tsp caster sugar

1 egg yolk

Champagne

In a cocktail shaker, place four ice cubes and add the brandy, Cointreau, cream, sugar and egg yolk. Shake well until frothy and creamy, and strain into a champagne flute, filling it to about the halfway mark. Carefully top up with chilled champagne.

Note: Because of the raw egg content, this drink should not be served to pregnant women or the elderly.

snappy apple fizz

You can make up any number of exciting cocktails by mixing fresh fruit juice with the spirit distilled from that juice. In this case we have used Calvados, which is apple brandy, with pure clear apple juice. The champagne turns it into a sparkling treat.

1 very ripe golden apple

1 cup Calvados

About ½ cup clear, still apple juice

Champagne

Peel and core the apple and cut into neat slices. Place the slices in a shallow bowl or saucer, cover with Calvados and leave in the fridge overnight to soak. When ready to serve, place a slice of the soaked apple in each champagne flute and cover with the calvados. Add apple juice to half fill the glass. Carefully top with chilled champagne.

fuzzy peach

This cocktail follows the style of the Snappy Apple Fizz (see page 134), but uses peaches and peach schnapps instead of apple and calvados.

1 ripe yellow peach

1 cup peach schnapps

1 cup peach juice or purée

Champagne

Peel the peach, remove the stone and cut into thin slices. Place the slices in a shallow bowl or cup, cover with peach schnapps and store overnight in the fridge. When ready to serve, place a slice of peach in each champagne flute and cover with the peach schnapps. Add the peach juice or purée to half fill the glass. Carefully top up with chilled champagne.

blue champagne cocktail

We hardly ever eat or drink anything that is blue, so a blue drink always has a dramatic impact. A clever barman always keeps a bottle of blue curaçao handy to add glamour to a drink. Just a few drops will do the trick.

Ice cubes

1 bar measure (about 30 ml/1 fl oz) vodka

Juice of ½ lemon

Splash of triple sec

Dash of blue cucaçao

Champagne

Place four or five ice cubes in a cocktail shaker, add the vodka, lemon juice, triple sec and curaçao. Shake well and strain into a champagne flute, to about a quarter full. Carefully top up with champagne. Obviously, the intensity of the colour can be regulated by adjusting the quantity of blue curaçao used.

fuzzy navel

The Fuzzy Navel is one of the timeless classics of the cocktail world and consists of Peach Schnapps and orange juice. All it takes is a good splash of dry champagne to turn it into a tall, summer evening refresher. It is sometimes called a Fizzy Fuzzy Navel.

Ice cubes

About 1 sherry-glass of peach schnapps

The same quantity of freshly squeezed orange juice

Brut champagne

Place three or four ice cubes in a tall glass and pour in the peach schnapps and orange juice to fill the glass about one-third full. Top up gently with chilled champagne and stir very lightly, taking care not to disperse the bubbles. If you prefer a less alcoholic drink, double the orange juice and halve the peach schnapps.

london bus

Several drinks have the name London in their titles, sometimes for no apparent reason. Maybe that's where the drink was first served. This one balances the sweetness of mandarin juice with the tartness of grapefruit.

1 bar measure (about 30 ml/1 fl oz) mandarin juice

1 bar measure (about 30 ml/1 fl oz) grapefruit juice

1 tsp grenadilla syrup

Champagne

Simply pour the fruit juices and syrup into a chilled champagne flute, stir and gently add the champagne to fill.

corpse reviver

I have come across several cocktail recipes that call themselves corpse revivers. Maybe there's more than one way to revive a corpse. What they have in common is that all of them are claimed to be quick cures for hangovers.

1 tsp lemon juice

1 bar measure (about 30 ml/1 fl oz) Pernod or other anise liqueur

Brut champagne

Pour the lemon juice into a champagne flute and add the Pernod. Carefully top up the glass with chilled champagne.

rossini

Champagne and strawberries are the trademark delights of Wimbledon week, so this may be the perfect drink to sip while watching the titans battle on Centre Court – preferably from the comfort of your favourite armchair in front of the telly.

Bowl of fresh strawberries

Dry champagne

Purée some of the strawberries and pour into a chilled champagne flute, filling it to the halfway mark. Carefully top up with chilled champagne and float a whole strawberry on top.

green dream

Everybody's going green these days and the splash of Midori melon liqueur adds a merry green touch to this celebratory drink. If made carefully it should have separate layers of colour.

1 bar measure (about 30 ml/1 fl oz) Midori melon liqueur

1 bar measure (about 30 ml/1 fl oz) vodka

Dash of Rose's lime juice cordial

Champagne

Starting with the Midori, add the ingredients gently, one by one, in a champagne flute, trying to mix them as little as possible. Follow the Midori with the vodka, then the lime juice and finally the chilled champagne.

champagne napoleon

Mandarine Napoleon is a brandy-based liqueur flavoured with the dried skins of the mandarin commun. It adds an exotic touch to this elegant drink. If you are unable to obtain Mandarine Napoleon, you may substitute the South African liqueur known as Van Der Hum.

1 bar measure (about 30 ml/1 fl oz) Mandarine Napoleon

Generous splash of fresh orange juice

Champagne

Pour the Mandarine Napoleon into a champagne flute, add the orange juice but do not stir. Top up gently with chilled champagne.

bubbly london buck

The classic London Buck cocktail is made using ginger ale to add sparkle. This one uses an off-dry champagne or sparkling wine instead.

1 bar measure (about 30 ml/1 fl oz) London dry gin

Juice of ½ lemon

Five ice cubes

Demi-sec champagne, spumante or other sparkling wine

Twist of lemon rind, to garnish

Stir the gin and lemon juice together well, fill a highball glass with ice cubes and pour the gin and lemon over them. Top up with the sparkling wine. You may wish to decorate the drink with a twist of lemon rind.

green fizz

The addition of egg white into a shaken drink adds a pretty silvery sheen to it. Add this to a fresh green colour and you have a very pretty drink indeed.

Ice cubes

1 bar measure (about 30 ml/1 fl oz) London dry gin

Juice of ½ lemon

3 dashes of green crème de menthe

Splash of sugar syrup

1 egg white

Brut champagne

Place four or five ice cubes in a cocktail shaker and add all the ingredients except the champagne. Fill a highball glass with ice, shake the cocktail well and strain it over the ice in the glass. Top with chilled brut.

Note: Because of the raw egg content, this drink should not be served to pregnant women or the elderly.

cherry fizz

There are several versions of this merry cherry drink, and some use club soda instead of champagne. That's fine if you want to economise, but why not splash out and spoil yourself?

Ice cubes

1 bar measure (about 30 ml/1 fl oz) cherry brandy

Juice of ½ lemon

Champagne

2 cocktail cherries, to garnish

Place three or four ice cubes in a cocktail shaker and add the cherry brandy and lemon juice. Shake well, strain into a highball glass and top up with chilled champagne. Decorate with two cocktail cherries on a stick.

chicago fizz royale

Any drink with the word royale in the title is likely to contain champagne, because champagne is the acknowledged king of wines. Chicago Fizz is usually spritzed up with club soda, but a generous helping of brut champagne adds the crown.

Ice cubes

1 Tbsp Jamaica rum

1 Tbsp ruby port

Juice of ½ lemon

1 egg white

1 tsp caster sugar

Champagne

Place four ice cubes in a cocktail shaker and add the rum, port, lemon juice, egg white and caster sugar. Shake very well, strain into a tall glass and carefully top up with chilled champagne.

Note: Because of the raw egg content, this drink should not be served to pregnant women or the elderly.

silk 'n' silver

An egg white shaken into a cocktail gives it a pretty silken sheen, which is why this cocktail got its name.

Ice cubes

1 egg white

2 tsp dry gin

2 tsp dark rum

Dash of sugar syrup

2 tsp lemon juice

Brut champagne

Place four ice cubes in a cocktail shaker and add the egg white, gin, rum, sugar syrup and lemon juice. Shake very well and strain into a highball glass. Top with Brut champagne.

Note: Because of the raw egg content, this drink should not be served to pregnant women or the elderly.

funapple

There's a non-alcoholic version of this delicious drink, which uses rum essence and apple juice. We feel the alcoholic version puts more fun into a Funapple.

Crushed ice

Dash of Angostura bitters

1 bar measure (about 30 ml/1 fl oz) dark rum

1 bar measure (about 30 ml/1 fl oz) apple cider

Champagne

Slice of apple, to garnish

Fill a tall highball glass with crushed ice, add a couple of dashes of bitters and pour in the rum and apple cider. Top with champagne and decorate with a slice of apple.

garden party

This simple but exciting cocktail uses a Finnish liqueur called Vaapukka, made from raspberries.

1 bar measure (about 30 ml/1 fl oz) Vaapukka

Dry champagne

Fresh raspberry, to garnish (optional)

Pour the Vaapukka into a champagne flute and top with chilled champagne. In the unlikely event you have a fresh raspberry handy, pop it in as decoration.

lion's pride

The name of this cocktail gives no indication whether it refers to the pride of a single lion or his family, which is also his pride. Maybe it was just the glossy, tawny colour that reminded its inventor of a pride of lions.

Ice cubes

1 bar measure (about 30 ml/1 fl oz) Advokaat

1 Tbsp crème de banane

1 Tbsp lemon juice

Dash of crème de cacao

½ egg white

Champagne

Place four or five ice cubes in a cocktail shaker and add all the ingredients except the champagne. Shake well, strain into a champagne flute and top up with chilled champagne.

Note: Because of the raw egg content, this drink should not be served to pregnant women or the elderly.

party punches

champagne punch

Sadly, punch bowls are not as popular as they were in Victorian times, but they are still fun and guaranteed to create a friendly atmosphere – particularly when one of the ingredients of the punch is champagne. It takes a bit of effort to create a good punch, but it's worth every moment.

Glass of triple sec

Bottle of dark rum

Sherry-glass of maraschino liqueur

3 cups chilled pineapple juice

A large block of ice (or a cup of ice cubes)

Bottle of club soda

Bottle of ginger ale

4 bottles of champagne (any dry sparkling wine will do)

In a large punch bowl or tureen, combine the triple sec, rum, maraschino and pineapple juice. Place in the fridge for about 1 hour to allow the ingredients to combine well. Just before serving, place a block of ice in the centre of the bowl and add the club soda, ginger ale and champagne. Stir gently and serve, traditionally in small punch cups, but wine glasses will do well.

glayva champagne punch

Glayva is a Scottish whisky-based liqueur with added flavours of herbs and spices. It adds a powerful flavour to this seriously strong punch.

Block of ice, or large ice cubes

1 cup Glayva

1 cup brandy

1 cup maraschino

2 cups caster sugar

Large bottle of sparkling mineral water

2 bottles of champagne

Fruits in season

Place a block of ice in a punch-bowl and add the Glayva, brandy, maraschino and sugar. Stir well to dissolve the sugar and then add the sparkling mineral water. Finally, add the champagne and float chunks of washed and peeled fruit in the bowl.

iced bishop punch

I have no idea why this drink was consecrated a bishop. Maybe the dignity of the lemon tea added a serious note to it.

2 cups lemon tea, chilled

1 cup brandy

1 cup gomme syrup

1 orange, sliced

1 lemon, sliced

Ice cubes

Bottle of champagne

Mix the chilled lemon tea, brandy, gomme syrup and slices of fruit in a punch bowl with 2 cups of ice cubes. Stir well. When ready to serve, add the chilled champagne.

independence day punch

Most of the ingredients in this merry punch are from France, so it would probably be an appropriate drink to serve at a Bastille Day celebration. One friend served it to mark the end of an unhappy marriage. He claimed to be celebrating his own independence.

2 cups caster sugar

3 bottles of claret

One bottle of Cognac (or any brandy)

3 cups lemon juice

Six sliced lemons

Ice cubes

1 bottle of champagne

Simply mix all the ingredients, with the exception of the champagne, in a large punch bowl. Stir well and add the chilled champagne just before serving.

fiesta royale punch

Here's another delicious punch usually made using soda water, but improved a great deal by adding champagne. In this case a sweeter sparkling wine might be the ideal one to use.

Caster sugar, to taste

1 cup unsweetened pineapple juice

Juice of 2 lemons

1 bottle of sweet white wine

Large block of ice

1 bottle of off-dry champagne

Slices of pineapple

Dissolve the caster sugar in the pineapple juice and add the lemon juice and sweet wine. Place the block of ice in a punch bowl, pour in the wine-fruit mixture, carefully add the champagne and float slices of pineapple in the bowl.

champagne
peach punch

It makes sense to use any fruit that is in season, particularly if you have your own fruit tree. This cheerful party punch is ideal for a summer evening gathering of friends when the peaches are ripe.

Dozen large ripe peaches

¼ cup lemon juice

¼ cup grenadine syrup

½ cup peach brandy or peach schnapps

Ice cubes

Large (750 ml/26 fl oz) bottle of soda water

3 bottles of champagne

Peel and stone the peaches and purée to a smooth creamy texture. Place the purée in a large punch bowl and add the lemon juice, grenadine syrup and brandy or schnapps. When ready to serve add 2 cups of ice cubes, stir well, then pour in the soda water and finally add the champagne.

rocky mountain punch

This intriguing punch recipe comes from a delightful book called Table Topics, published in London in the 1950s. The recipe says the quantities are sufficient 'for a mixed party of twenty'. It gives the impression it was written for a more opulent age.

1 quart (about 1 litre/ 35 fl oz, but say one bottle) Jamaica rum

About ½ litre (1 pint) maraschino

Sugar, to taste

Six lemons, sliced

Large block of ice

5 bottles of champagne

In a large punch bowl mix the rum, maraschino, sugar and lemons together and allow to stand overnight if possible. Before serving, place a large block of ice in the centre of the bowl and pour in the champagne, stirring it gently.

lemon sorbet punch

A punch bowl adds a refreshing and elegant touch to a summer lunch party. This one should serve about a dozen guests in grand style. The lemon flavours make it crisp and cooling. To make a pineapple version of this drink, follow the note below.

1 litre (35 fl oz) lemon sorbet

1 tsp Angostura bitters

2 bottles of chilled champagne

2 lemons, sliced

Place the lemon sorbet in a large punch bowl and add the bitters. Crush the sorbet and slowly pour the champagne over it. Finish by floating a few slices of lemon in the bowl before serving.

Note: For a Pineapple Sorbet Punch, substitute pineapple sorbet for the lemon and add slices of fresh pineapple instead of the lemon slices.

sangria especiale

Sangria is a popular drink in warm Mediterranean climates and the basic recipe consists of red wine and orange juice, served in a glass with a sugar-frosted rim. To turn it into an 'especiale' just add champagne. Be warned that this is a highly alcoholic drink and not to be served to anybody under 18 years old. Anybody planning to drive home afterwards is also advised to steer clear.

Ice cubes

2 bottles of red wine

1 bottle of brut champagne

1 wine-glass of gin

1 wine-glass of Cognac

Juice of 3 oranges

Juice of 2 lemons

Sugar, to taste

Orange and lemon slices, to garnish

Simply place a few cups of ice cubes in a large punch bowl and add all the ingredients, except the sugar. Stir gently and taste, adding sugar until it is perfectly balanced – sweet and sour. Garnish with slices of orange and lemon, and serve in wine glasses, using a soup ladle.

index

absinthe: Death in the Afternoon 100
Advokaat: Lion's Pride 166
Alfonso 88
Amaretto Ritz 114
Americana 104
Angostura bitters: Alfonso 88
    Champagne Normande 86
    Classic Champagne Cocktail 90
    Funapple 162
    Lemon Sorbet Punch 184
    London Special 94
    Prince of Wales 116
apple juice: Snappy Apple Fizz 134

Bellini 92
Black Velvet 72
Blue Champagne Cocktail 138
Bollinger, Lily 8, 11, 41
bourbon: Americana 104
    Imperial Fizz 106
brandy: Brunch Bubbly 74
    Champagne Flip 132
    Champagne Julep 84
    Classic Champagne Cocktail 90
    D'Artagnan 126
    Glayva Champagne Punch 172
    Iced Bishop Punch 174
    Independence Day Punch 176
    Prince of Wales 116
Brunch Bubbly 74
Bubbly London Buck 152
Buck's Fizz 68

Calvados: Champagne Normande 86
    Snappy Apple Fizz
Caribbean Champagne 80
Chambord: Chambord Royal Spritzer 102
    Ruby Royale 82

champagne: bottle 18–19
  brands 44
  cellar tours 43–45
  and food 24, 46–50
  grape varieties 15, 18
  history 12–14
  to open 31–34
  process 18–21
  region 14, 43
  sabrage 35–38
  sugar content 21
  widows 39–41
Champagne Chicken Breasts 58
Champagne Flip 132
Champagne Ham Glaze 60
Champagne Julep 84
Champagne Martini 76
Champagne Napoleon 150
Champagne Normande 86
Champagne Oysters 56
Champagne, Peach and
  Melon Soup 54
Champagne Peach Punch 180
Champagne Punch 170
Champear 122
Cherry Fizz 156
Chicago Fizz Royale 158
Chicken Breasts, Champagne
  58
cider: Funapple 162
claret: Independence Day
Punch 176
Classic Champagne Cocktail
  90
Clicquot Ponsardin, Barbe
Nicole 39–40
Cognac: Classic Champagne
  Cocktail 90

Eve 108
Independence Day Punch 176
King's Peg 110
Prince of Wales 116
Royal Screw 130
Sangria Especiale 186
Cointreau: Champagne Flip
  132
Corpse Reviver 144
cranberry juice: Poinsettia 124
crème de banane: Caribbean
  Champagne 80
  Lion's Pride 166
crème de cacao: Lion's Pride
  166
crème de cassis: Kir Royal 70
crème de menthe: Green Fizz
  154
curaçao: Amaretto Ritz 114
  Blue Champagne Cocktail
    138
  Eve 108
  Prince of Wales 116

D'Artagnan 126
Death in the Afternoon 100
Dubonnet: Alfonso 88

egg: Champagne Flip 132
  Chicago Fizz Royale 158
  Green Fizz 154
  Lion's Pride 166
  Silk 'n' Silver 160
Eve 108

Fiesta Royale Punch 178
French 75 128
Funapple 162

Fuzzy Navel 140
Fuzzy Peach 136

Garden Party 164
The Ghost 120
gin: Bubbly London Buck 152
    French 75 128
    Green Fizz 154
    Sangria Especiale 186
    Silk 'n' Silver 160
ginger ale: Champagne Punch
    170
Glayva Champagne Punch 172
gomme syrup: Iced Bishop
    Punch 174
Grand Marnier: D'Artagnan
    126
grapefruit juice: London Bus
    142
Green Dream 148
Green Fizz 154
grenadilla syrup: London Bus
    142
grenadine syrup: Champagne
    Peach Punch 180
Guinness: Black Velvet 72

Ham Glaze, Champagne 60

Iced Bishop Punch 174
Imperial Fizz 106
Independence day Punch 176

King's Peg 110
Kir Royal 78

Laurent-Perrier, Mathilde Emile
    40

lemon juice: Amaretto Ritz 114
    Blue Champagne Cocktail
    138
    Bubbly London Buck 152
    Champagne Peach Punch
    180
    Cherry Fizz 154
    Corpse Reviver 144
    Fiesta Royale Punch 178
    French 75 128
    Green Fizz 154
    Imperial Fizz 106
    Independence Day Punch
    176
    Lion's Pride 166
    Silk 'n' Silver 160
Lemon Sorbet Punch 184
lemon tea: Iced Bishop Punch
    174
lime juice cordial: Green
Dream 148
Lion's Pride 166
London Bus 142
London Special 94

Madeira: Prince of Wales 116
mandarin juice: London Bus
    142
Mandarine Napoleon:
Champagne Napoleon 150
maraschino liqueur:
Champagne Punch 170
    Glayva Champagne Punch
    172
    Rocky Mountain Punch 182
Midori melon liqueur: The
    Ghost 120
    Green Dream 148

Mimosa 98

Nelson's Blood 96
Nonancourt, Marie-Louise de 40

Olry-Roederer, Camille 41
orange bitters: Americana 104
    Caribbean Champagne 80
orange juice: Buck's Fizz 68
    Champagne Napoleon 150
    D'Artagnan 126
    Fuzzy Navel 140
    Mimosa 98
    Royal Screw 130
Oysters, Champagne 56

peach brandy: Champagne
    Peach Punch 180
peach juice: Bellini 92
    Brunch Bubbly 74
    Fuzzy Peach 136
peach schnapps: Champagne
    Peach Punch 180
    Fuzzy Navel 140
    Fuzzy Peach 136
pear brandy: Champear 122
    Tintoretto 112
Pérignon, Dom 12–14
Pernod: Corpse Reviver 144
    Death in the Afternoon 100
    Eve 108
Pimm's Royal 118
pineapple juice: Champagne
    Punch 170
    Fiesta Royale Punch 178
Poinsettia 124
Pomegranate Sorbet with
    Bubbles 62

Pommery, Louise 40
port, ruby: Chicago Fizz
    Royale 158
port, tawny: Nelson's Blood 96
Prince of Wales 116

raspberries: Champagne
Martini 76
    Ruby Royale 82
Rocky Mountain Punch 182
Rossini 146
Royal Screw 130
Ruby Royale 82
rum, dark: Champagne Punch
    170
    Funapple 162
    Rocky Mountain Punch 182
    Silk 'n' Silver 160
rum, Jamaica: Chicago Fizz
    Royale 158
rum, white: Caribbean
Champagne 80

Sangria Especiale 186
Silk 'n' Silver 160
Snappy Apple Fizz 134
soda water: Champagne
    Peach Punch 180
Sorbet, Pomegranate, with
    Bubbles 62
Soup, Champagne, Peach
    and Melon 54
strawberries: Brunch Bubbly 74
    Rossini 146

Tangerine Treat 78
Tintoretto 112
triple sec: Blue Champagne

Cocktail 138
  Champagne Punch 170
  Mimosa 98
  Poinsettia 124

Vaapukka: Garden Party 164
vodka: Blue Champagne
Cocktail 138
  Champagne Martini 76
  Green Dream 148
  Ruby Royale 82

wine, red: Sangria Especiale
  186
wine, sparkling 11, 14–15
  process 27–30
wine, white: Fiesta Royale
Punch 178
winemaking process 9–11

PICTURE CREDITS

pages 6–7 and 42: Bollinger
page 12: © Stefano Bianchetti/Corbis;
page 23: © Schlegelmilch/Corbis;
page 46: © Bettmann/Corbis